I'll be Okay

Jimmy Tran

Contents

It's okay.

Everyone's journey is different.

Everyone's life is different.

I hope even in your darkest days,

You find the will to keep moving on.

I don't know what life you've lived,

But I hope you will make it out.

Your voice matters.

Your story matters.

Your life matters.

Give yourself time.

You don't have to believe me.

That's okay.

But I hope you'll be okay.

Behind My Smile

I wear my smile every day

But sometimes it doesn't feel like me

I wear my smile to the show

But I don't think you'll ever know

I wear it to hide me from you

From a world you will never see.

What do you see behind my smile?

Do you see the anger building inside of me?

Do you see my face twist?

Do you see my eyes widen with excitement?

What do you see?

Because that's not me.

What do you see behind my smile?

Do you see the anger unfold?

Do you see the hatred in my face?

Do you see the light fade from my eyes?

What do you see?

Because that's not me.

What do you see behind my smile?

Do you see their blood on my cheek?

Do you see my blackened eye?

Do you see the bruises on my face?

What do you see?

Because that's not me.

What do you see behind my smile?

Do you see the senseless joy on my face?

Do you see my unbridled excitement?

Do you see my hellish smile?

What do you see?

Because that's not me.

What do you see behind my smile?

Do you see the light return to my eyes?

Do you see the anguish strike me?

Do you see the emptiness fill me?

What do you see?

Because that's me.

My smile belongs to the scarecrow

The one that has taken my place

My smile has been chained inside

The stone coffin of my heart

I buried it deep within

So that you will never have to see

The monster that lives inside of me.

What was I supposed to feel?

Ever since I was young

In spite of my best attempts

The question has long plagued my mind

What am I supposed to feel?

What was I supposed to feel?

When I was doing poorly in school

I didn't care

It didn't matter to me

I wasn't happy or sad

I was indifferent

Despite what they were telling me

What was I supposed to feel?

When I was doing well in school

I didn't care

It didn't matter to me

The happiness that was felt

Didn't come from me

It came from the people around me

What was I supposed to feel?

When I was surrounded with people

It didn't matter to me

No amount of laughter

No amount of time spent together

Could change the emptiness in my chest.

I was a ghost in my own head.

What was I supposed to feel?

When their soft voices reached out for me

It didn't matter to me.

The sweet words that came from my lips were empty

The laughter and smiles held nothing behind them

I clung to the warmth of another's arms

Unable to feel anything but the cold inside

What was I supposed to feel?

When I was alone

It didn't matter to me

The deafening silence

Trapped in a coffin of my own thoughts

It didn't change the emptiness in my chest

I was a corpse in my own head.

What was I supposed to feel?

When the chips fell

I could finally feel my heart beat.

The adrenaline coursing in my veins

The excitement I felt

Hit me again

I need to feel my heart race

How else am I supposed to feel alive?

When my vices took control

I flooded my body

Just to keep the feeling

Remind me I'm a person.

Remind me I'm alive.

I need to feed this feeling

How else am I supposed to live?

When the world came tumbling down

And the pain clawed at my body

Perhaps it was better that I wasn't alive.

Perhaps the numbness was better.

Perhaps it was better that I didn't feel

Cause it wouldn't have turned out this way.

What was I supposed to feel?

Since those days

Despite my best attempts

The thoughts have plagued my mind

Maybe it was better this way.

Maybe the emptiness was alright.

Because I don't have to feed the frenzy

To know I am alive.

Am I too much?

Am I too much?

Was my smile too bright?

Did my laughter cut the inside of your ears?

How did it make you feel to see me?

What was it about my happiness that you hated?

Why did you make that face?

Who was I to make you turn away?

Am I too much?

Was what I did not okay?

Did my words cut you?

How did my hands feel against your skin?

What was it that surprised you?

Why did you look at me like that?

Who was I to make you turn away?

Am I too much?

Was the sound of crushing bone too loud?

Did the sight of me terrify you?

How did you feel when you saw me?

What was it about my anger that made you shake like that?

Why did you run from me?

Who was I to make you turn away?

Am I too much?

Was the blood on my knuckles horrifying?

Did my broken voice make you retch?

How did you close the door on me?

What was it that disgusted you?

Why did you leave me?

Who was I to make you turn away?

Am I too much?

Was the monster that filled you with fear me?

Did I haunt you at night?

How did I not see how you felt about me?

What could I do to make you stay?

Why would you leave me?

Who was I to make you turn away?

Am I too much?

Were my feelings too much of a burden?

Did I make you feel the same way I do now?

How did you ever stay?

What have I done?

Why does this hurt so much?

Who was I to make you turn away?

Happiness was within reach

The surprise you felt was because you never saw me

My anger was never aimed at you

But you had every right to be disgusted

But you had every right to fear me

But the sadness is what brought me back.

Please Help Me

Please help me.

This loneliness, this emptiness,

It's eating me away.

My heart is restless, my lungs are breathless

I can't get it out of my head

It's buried itself deep into my heart

Please help me.

I am tumbling, I am crumbling

I feel like I am wasting away.

My body doesn't want to move on.

My legs don't want to carry on.

I can't forgive myself

It is etched into my thoughts.

Please help me.

The mistakes are piling, I feel like I'm dying

I am reaching for the light when everything is already gray

My eyes are so faded, my heart feels so jaded

I want to bury myself away.

My heart won't stop breaking day-by-day

Please help me.

The smile is fading, my days are wasting

I don't want to be here today.

I don't want to be myself today.

I don't want to look at what I've done today.

Why won't anyone look at me today?

I want to cry it all away.

Please help me.

This loneliness is killing me

The smiling faces won't stop looking at me

The ghost of who I am

Won't forgive me for who I was.

Please won't anyone help me?

All of these faces feel meaningless.

When there is no one left for me.

Who is supposed to reach out to me?

Please save me.

No one hears me.

No one wants to listen to me.

No one wants to listen to what I have to say.

My voice is fading, my heart is aching.

The characters of my own mind feel surreal.

It's only in them that someone wants to listen to me.

They are not real. They are what I wish for.

They are not real. They are who I want to be.

They are not real. They are all in my mind.

Please, won't anyone save me?

I know it's just the loneliness.

No matter who I surround myself with,

It still feels like no one is on my side.

No matter how many friends I'm told I have,

It doesn't feel like anyone is reaching out for me.

No matter what I do,

It doesn't feel like anyone wants to talk to me.

Not for me.

I'm tired.

I don't want to do this anymore.

I'm making mistake after mistake.

That smile, it's a lie.

It's not for me. It's not for anyone.

They're not real.

There's nothing left of me.

Weight

Everyone carries their own weight

It comes in many shapes and forms.

I lumbered around with my wagon

Happily collecting everything that I wanted

It wasn't a lot

But it was mine.

No matter how small it was

I was happy to call it mine.

There was no direction

There was no goal

I wasn't building anything

I wasn't building a collection

Just an assortment of things

That made me smile

That was enough for me.

Then one day,

Someone asked me to watch their tree.

It was tall

It was heavy

It was firmly planted in the ground

After that day,

I never left that shadow.

No matter how far it felt like I stumbled

No matter where I tried to hide

No matter how I tried to sprint to the sun

I couldn't escape its shadow

It always seemed to loom overhead.

When they can't take care of it anymore

Who will?

It was theirs.

I don't want it to die.

I don't want it to get dirty.

I don't want it to fade away.

I tried pushing it

I tried pulling it

I tried lifting it

I didn't want to leave it

But I couldn't carry it in my wagon

I pulled with all my might.

It was too heavy.

My arms felt like they were breaking

The small things inside my wagon shattered

The wheels broke down

Eventually my fingers gave out

And I fell to the ground.

My wagon was crushed behind me

As the weight of it all crashed down.

I tried my best to pull the wagon from the wreckage

Picking up the small remnants

Of what once made me smile

But I couldn't get my wagon out.

I lashed out at the tree

Violently slashing and bashing it

Until my arms snapped

Scratching and biting at it

Until my nails and teeth bled

I collapsed, tears streaming down my face.

The weight of it

Was far more than what I could imagine.

The weight of it

Was far more than what I could carry.

The weight of it

Was far more than what I could handle.

I didn't know what to do.

I didn't know how to keep going.

I didn't know what I should do.

I didn't know how to pick up my stuff.

I didn't know why I should.

I ran

I ran as far as my legs could go

I ran as far as my thoughts would let me

I ran as far as my lungs could take

I ran as far as my heart could take

Until I collapsed under my own weight.

Prison of My Own Creation

Iridescent waves ebb and flow

Drifting onto the golden coastline

Spanning as far as I could see

A wonderful view I admired

From between the cracks

Of my own portcullis

Of my own prison

As I clutch the key in my hands.

Gray walls and dreary cells

Stretched into the empty void

Harrowing whispers echoed in the dark

A familiarity that was all I allowed myself to know

Writhing in my eyes and ears

From the comfort of my cell

From the world I created

As I clutch the key in my hands.

Warped visages and howling words

Nightmares of my past forged by my hands

Their likeness one I no longer feared

Their twisted smiles and bloodied eyes

Occupied the cells around me

Ones I could not let go

Ones I refused to let go

As I clutch the key in my hands.

From the gilded sands

Their shadows closed in

Willingly bringing themselves to my abode

Bright smiles beyond the cold steel

Joking and laughing with me

Their voices infectious

Their joy a virus

As I clutch the key in my hands.

I watch them drift down the golden coast

Their hopeful gaze turning back to meet mine

As I wave them goodbye another day

They belong to a world outside of my reach

Far past the grim hands that I craved

It's better this way.

It's safer this way.

As I clutch the key in my hands.

From the homey feeling of my cell
Against the cold lifeless metal grates
I continue to build my own monsters
Shaping them into my thoughts
Into voices and faces I wish to see
They can't hurt me this way
They won't be hurt by me this way
As I clutch the key in my hands.

The stars dot the sapphire sky
As I watch from my prison
Staring outside the gate that I made
The fiendish voices and faces
All I let myself know
Because it feels like home

Because I'm scared of who I am

As I stare at the key in my hands.

In My Dreams

In my dreams where I died,

You were never by my side.

Even in the darkest of nights,

When you lay by my side,

I never felt so alone when I closed my eyes.

In the dreams where I died,

In an iron coffin, water filling my lungs.

I never reached out for your hand.

I let the coffin overflow

I let myself sink.

I let the broken glass and metal pierce my flesh and bone.

But I remember your hand was reaching out for me.

In the dreams where I died,

Far above the clouds, feet dangling in the breeze.

I waited to make sure you would never catch me.

I let the wind embrace me.

I let the world collect me.

I let the crimson ichor pour from me.

But I remember seeing your eyes as I drifted off.

In the dreams where I died,

In the silence of my home, letting my thoughts suffocate me.

I could hear you at my door.

I let myself cry.

I let myself shout.

I let the bullet out.

But I remember hearing you scream.

In the dreams where I died,

In the darkness of the city, blood streaming from my side.

I could hear your engine grow closer

I let myself fall to the ground

I let myself twist and turn

I let myself hurt

But I remember your lights flooding the alley.

In the dreams where I died,

Stumbling across a field of flowers, painting the petals red.

I could see you chasing after me

I let myself collapse

I let myself stare at the clouds

I let myself fade away.

But I remember the way your hands felt.

In the dreams where I died,

You were always chasing me.

Even in the darkest times,

You were running through the dark,

To tell me that I was never alone.

Lost in the Snow

In the coldest of winters,

I was a rampaging monster,

Hunting anything that peered out from the snow,

Slashing and crashing into everything around me

In a wretched, lucid dream.

Please run from me.

Please make that face again.

Please make me bleed again.

The fear in your eyes was intoxicating.

The taste of my own blood was exhilarating.

The pain makes me feel alive.

I want to make you bleed.

I want you to make me bleed.

I don't want this pain to end.

In the shade of the frozen trees,

I was a shambling zombie

Scraping my flesh from bone,

And drinking my sickly sweet blood,

Just to feel alive again.

Please look at me.

Please give me more.

Please feed the poison in my veins.

The disgusting look on your face,

The crooked smile that formed on your twisted mug,

The malice unveiled in your eyes.

I didn't care enough.

I didn't want to care.

I only care about the venom inside me.

In the loneliest of nights,

I became a corpse buried in snow,

Watching the color fade from my limbs,

Feeling the light fade from my eyes,

As the crows fed on my body.

Please don't look at me.

Please don't give me your pity.

Please let me go into the endless night.

The venom has long left me.

The pain remains buried deep in my bones.

The ghosts have caught up to me.

I don't want to be here anymore.

I don't want to try anymore.

I don't want to live anymore.

In the silence of my coffin,

I was ripped away from my slumber

Feeling a long-forgotten warmth

Underneath my barren bones

As you desperately tried to put me together.

Please don't look at me like that.

Please leave me alone.

Please let me go.

The soft touch of your voice is too much for me to bear

The pain is too much for me to bear

The warmth is too much for me to bear

I don't want to hurt you.

I don't want to need you.

I don't want you.

In the warmth of your home,

I was a husk, scared of my own shadow

Hiding away underneath gentle cloth

Fearful of the faintest touch

Upon my brittle body

Please don't look at me like that.

Please don't give me my heart back.

Please don't make me try again.

The warmth will shatter my body.

The ghosts won't let me rest.

The memories will claw into my skin.

I don't know if I can do it.

I don't know if I'll make it.

I don't know if I deserve to live.

In the calm of night,

I was scared of your kindness

Vanishing into the snow once more

My rotten flesh given warmth once more

My heart beating in my chest once more.

Please don't look for me.

Please don't hurt yourself for me.

Please take care of yourself.

The warmth you gave me is still there

The kindness you showed me is still there

The soft smile you showed me is still there

I don't know how long the winter will last.

I don't know when I'll be back.

I don't know if I'll be back.

But I know the winter will end.

But I know I will make it through the snow.

But I know I will make it out of the forest.

Because I want to see the blue sky you told me of.

Because I want to see the flowers spring from the snow.

Because I want to see the future you were painting.

And, sometimes, that's enough of a reason.

Cold Fingers

My cold fingers once reached out for you

A mangled body before my feet

Broken and beaten by ill fate

Limbs strewn about in disarray

Letting the warm crimson cover me.

My cold fingers once held you

A piece of my heart clenched in my arms

Bloodied and limp by what we've done

Skin becoming cold to the touch

But the warmth wouldn't stop.

My cold fingers once reached out to you

A part of me lifted to the skies

Buried underneath packed dirt

Your face never to be seen again

But the life you lived never lost.

My cold fingers once reached for the phone

A part of me was missing

Broken and lost

Your name on the top of the screen

But you never picked up.

My cold fingers once reached for glass

A part of me had died

By what had happened

You would never be back

But I never forgot who you were.

My cold fingers once reached for the phone

A part of me hopeful

But I knew you wouldn't pick up

You couldn't and I knew

But I couldn't stop myself.

My cold fingers once dropped the phone

A part of me terrified

By what I heard

There was someone else there

And I was never going to be the same.

Underneath the Stars

Underneath the stars,

The pain crawling through my veins

My fingers numb to the touch

My hands bleeding and bruised

My head dulled to my thoughts

The stars above seem so far away.

Underneath the stars,

The cold wind brushing my cheeks

My face numb to the touch

My hands cutting through the breeze

My head rushing with a thousand thoughts

The stars above look so small yet so bright.

Underneath the stars,

The silence of my room was deafening

My face wet to the touch

My hands trembling when I saw your name

My head thundering when I thought of you

The stars shone through the darkness.

Underneath the stars,

The door flung open

My face bursting open with a thunderous roar

My hands clenching until I bleed

My head desperate to escape itself

The stars seemed to glow brighter than ever.

Underneath the stars,

The clouds slowly fading away

My face twisting and turning with every thought

My hands crawling inside my hair

My head pounding, echoing to my bones

The stars were my beacon in the dark.

Underneath the stars,

The sunlight slowly began to break through

My face drying ever so slowly

My hands falling by my side

My head clutching the brakes

The stars were leaving my sight.

Under the sun,

The cold of the night had finally faded

My face couldn't feel the deathly sting

My hands unfurled

My head empty, eyes listlessly forward

The night was finally over.

Under the sun,

I didn't know what to do

I couldn't look back

My hands reached out for whatever was in front of me

My head desperately searched for a way forward

Because my night was over.

A Castle of Sand

When we were kids,

My parents used to take us to the beach a lot.

We'd wade in the waters

Play in the sand

Chase each other across the horizon

Laugh, scream, and fight each other.

Then one day,

My parents handed me a bucket and shovel

And asked if I could build a castle of sand

I didn't know what I was doing

But I didn't want to let them down.

My parents would guide me on what to do

Taught me how to do the basics

It was messy at first

The water kept swallowing it bit by bit

What worked for them didn't work for me.

I started to build what I wanted

With the sticks, stones, and shells I picked up around me

It started to look alright to me.

It didn't make me happy.

It didn't make me sad.

Then the waves became higher than they used to be

Was I angry or was I sad?

I screamed out at the top of my lungs

I knocked over what remained of my castle

It was the only thing I knew how to do.

I sat in the ruins

Water crashed around me

I buried my head in my hands

Screaming and sobbing

I wanted to give up.

Through my teary eyes, I looked down the beach

Everyone's castles looked different than mine

My brothers had made their own in their own way

It wasn't the prettiest

Sometimes it would topple over too.

But that didn't matter to my parents

They were happy

To see that they were trying on their own

While theirs was crumbling slowly with the wind

But they didn't seem to mind.

I picked up the tools I let the water carry away

And started to build again

Little by little

It started to look whole again

Broken here and there but it was alright.

People used to come by and help me

They don't come around as much as they used to

Sometimes their castles fell

And they never came back

Sometimes I scared them off

But that's okay.

A few of them built around me

They occasionally gave me shells to decorate the towers

Sometimes the towers I built would fall

Sometimes a seagull or a frisbee would knock them over

Sometimes it was me.

I would shout.

I would cry.

I would throw rocks at my castle.

I would knock it over.

I would let the water take it away.

Sometimes it would take me a long time to come back to it.

Sometimes I would let the water crash down around me.

Sometimes I would float on the water's surface.

Sometimes I would let myself sink

And let the water into my lungs.

But whenever I looked back at the sand

My parents would be standing there, a smile on their faces

My friends would have new decorations or food to share

My brothers would throw sand at me and ask me to play even when I didn't want to

But that would be enough for me to get up again.

My castle of sand looks okay

It doesn't have to be perfect.

It doesn't have to look great.

If something breaks, I can fix it again.

If it falls, I can make it again.

It's okay if it's not the prettiest.

It's okay if it's cracked.

It's okay if it's not the biggest.

It's okay if it's missing something.

It's okay if no one else likes it.

It just has to be mine

The ugly writing on the walls

The broken towers holding it up

The missing pieces hidden somewhere

The occasional footprint

This is my castle of sand

Hey Me of Yesterday

Hey me of yesterday,

It's been a while since we've talked.

Hey me of yesterday,

I know you have a lot going on.

Hey me of yesterday,

I know how you feel.

Hey me of yesterday,

I know you feel alone.

Hey me of yesterday,

I just want you to know I'm here.

I know it hurts.

I know that you're not angry.

I know you're trying your best in your own way.

I know that you're scared to be alone.

I know that you don't know another way.

It's okay for you to feel.

It's okay for you to take your time.

It's okay for you to take a break.

It's okay for you to cry.

It's okay.

The pain you feel is real

But it doesn't have to define you.

The anger you feel is a disguise you show

But it doesn't have to define you.

The scars you have are yours to bleed

But they will fade away.

The harrowing thoughts won't leave

But they won't be as loud.

The life you lived is yours

But the future is as well.

The clouds will give way for the stars

And you will see in front of you.

The rain will stop falling

And you can see how deep you were.

The mud will dry up

And you can pick your feet up.

The weight will lighten

And you can move forward.

The storm will end

And you'll survive it time and time again.

It's okay.

It's okay if you're not ready yet.

It's okay if you're not quite sure what to do.

It's okay if you take it one step at a time.

It's okay for you to follow your heart.

I know you will give it your all.

I know you will even if it makes you bleed.

I know you will even if it hurts.

I know you will once you find your smile.

I know you will once you find a reason to.

Hey me of yesterday,

It may seem tough, but I know you will make it.

Hey me of yesterday,

Don't give up on yourself yet.

Hey me of yesterday,

Don't give into the pain because it's all you've known.

Hey me of yesterday,

Give yourself another chance.

Hey me of yesterday,

It's okay if you mess up, but you have to get back up.

Hey me of yesterday,

I'm proud of you.

You survived another day.

www.ingramcontent.com/pod-product-compliance
Lightning Source LLC
La Vergne TN
LVHW090537110826
845146LV00003B/1139

9798987474983